YOU COME TOO

YOU COME TOO

Charles Schlee

Rev. date: 03/29/2019

To order additional copies of this book, contact:
Xlibris
1-888-795-4274
www.Xlibris.com
Orders@Xlibris.com
794635

CONTENTS

you come too

the sun is bright
the clouds are soft and few
mother said
you come too

the trees are tall
and some they look like drops of dew
mother said
you come too

rocks and lilies dot the path
and some they look like cows that moo
mother said
you come too

the earth is kind today
and some they look like birds that coo
mother said
you come too

we used to play before you left
mother didn't say just what to do
and now i only stop to bring you flowers
if only you'd come too

the pathway long and narrow

the pathway long and narrow
on which trod kings and mighty princes
as they conquered lands of all men's dreams
is now a home but to the sparrow

flowers blossoming along the roadside
birds pecking among rocks and seeds
in the beauty of a purple sunset
a child praying at her mother's knees

i saw a pathway long and narrow
now a home but to the sparrow

camels' caravans of wealth and riches
kegs of spices and choice wines
human chattel lean and dirty
brought by merchants from afar

i saw a pathway long and narrow
now a home but to the sparrow

the clanking wrath of roaring armies
conquering with caustic fervor
lavish realms of gold and silver
stuff that forms men's fondest hopes

i saw a pathway long and narrow
now a home but to the sparrow

o loathsome hand of him who tames
spare the rod by which thou came

be this our cry as we unfold
hidden deep within our souls
the once-tamed pathway long and narrow
now a home but to the sparrow

and be still me

noisy
happy
children were at play
they smiled
and laughed
in their unmeasured way

and they went on
and on they went
and on
they played
and on

there suddenly were voices
these voices did not play
these voices did but shout
berate
and take the fun away

and when the voices stopped
the children
did not smile
did not laugh
did not play
in their unmeasured way

some were sad
even crying
some were staring
others mad

and as i looked around
i could not help but see
there were no children now at play

i'd driven them away

then as i stood
and paused
i knew that
yes
i'd conquered
and depraved
yes i'd roared
i'd raged

yet couldn't help but ask
what was my conquest
what my victory
what did i take away

and even more
what did i leave
that it might grow
and live
and stay

so too i knew
by conquering
not leaving

i'd left myself behind

it was no longer i who lived
it was some other kind

where now was i
i who raged
i who shouted
drove away

and had i left
would i
before
behind
or in the middle
be

and be still me

the night

silent
and alone
i gaze into the darkness
of approaching
night

slowly
specks of light
begin to glimmer

soon
i start to feel
their distant call

and
for a while
i sit
and stare
and wonder

all at once
a pain cuts through my head
i languish
cry an air of loneliness

why am i apart
why am i still here
why am i not where i long to be
and what

and then i breathe
and feel the night without
within

and out i breathe my breath
and in the night
and out
and in
my breath
the night

wove now
into my deep drawn breath
the darkness seems a font of hope
it listens to my thoughts
it holds me as i overcome my doubts
it calms in my despair

soon i am at ease
as my pores receive
in gratitude
the grazing nearness
of the night air

her father's house

a girl
once showed me
her father's house

she showed me the living room
and said
here is where we sit and chat

she showed me the dining room
and said
here is where we eat our food

she showed me the kitchen
and said
here is where we cook our food

she showed me the library
and said
here is where we read our books

she showed me the game room
and said
here is where we play our games and have our fun

she showed me the bathroom
and said
here is where we take our baths

she showed me the bedroom
and said
here is where we sleep

and then i asked
but where do you make love

and she whispered
we make love
in the bedroom
under the covers
in the dark of night

and i said merely
oh

and then i remembered
that a great man once said
my father's house has many rooms
yet i say unto you

my father has no house

hymn to god the father

in nomine patris[1]
her eye caught the interstice
which crawled across the chapel wall
and on into the dull and ghastly hall

and with your spirit
she stood and drew more near it
she felt a beating pounding in her breast
of wrenching anguish and unrest

go the mass is ended
she saw a fleshless hand extended
which bled as from the heart of christ
she gasped
was this the price

---

[1] The opening words of this poem are taken from the Latin version of the Trinitarian formula: "in nomine Patris et Filii et Spiritus Sancti" ("in the name of the Father, and of the Son, and of the Holy Spirit").

unto dust

with unintended sympathy
i stretched my hand

head palmed
in rotund
exasperation
momently
with not a last
procrastination

in this brief concert of intensity
i took my stand

roses and daisies
the flowers
that i like
figure and motion
and spin
on my bike

that it might last for an eternity
like wind-tossed sand

grain to grist
flesh to dust
nor pulse
nor breath
like rod to rust

she whispered through this unity
i understand

the passing of a king

it is a drear evening
a barren table
would-be sculpting in the varnish
drifting lights
sinking through an open window

my son is leaving

i sit and watch the fire
as embers
turn to ash
are seen no more

soon we'll say farewell

i remember how when young
he'd run and jump on me
i'd hug him
kiss him
treat him like a king
as any loving father would his son

but times
as kings
are passing
these alone i saw

i know i'll miss him

from the dying fire
my weary eyes
wander to the window

there
i see an old man
walking through the park

he walks in silence
and alone
slowly
slightly hunched

though i know not
who he is
i feel i should

i stare
for quite some time
at his familiar gait

and wonder
who would walk
so slowly
and alone

and then
as he comes near
i see his face

my own

peter's lamentation

the cock crowed
while i forgot to say
i know you not

i was just so tired
the crowds
the dust
the jests
i guess i just forgot

but you forgave the adulteress
you cured the leper
you even loved a thief

i know i should have said
i know you not
but
well lord

i guess i just forgot

the gift

i had walked
alone
through the park
all that afternoon
until i saw her
just standing there
the sun's rays
gilding her silent gestures

i do not remember
exactly what we did
enshrined in our together
and aloneness
i think she raised her hand to wave
i think i smiled
i might have gently waved
i only know she came to me
and there
by the edge of a small creek
we met

it may have been
because we thought of it together
that we laughed
as we sat on the verdure

at the edge of the creek
removed our shoes
and let our feet
dangle in the cool water

then she bounced to her feet
glided across the soft turf
bent
and picked a dandelion

she turned
ran toward
reached out to me
the dandelion
resting on her open hand

i grazed her hand
so welcoming
soft
kind

then grasped her gift
and drew my hand away

when i looked up
there were but trees
and grass
and flowers
and the distant voices
of children at play

resurrection

i am nailed to a cross
through flesh
nerve
sinew
bone

i bleed
i hurt

the pain
it does not stop

i ache
can barely breathe

how can it be
that i should end
like this

and then
i see a boy

he looks at me

he holds my gaze
in his

and as he looks
i feel
a haven
somewhere
there
outside my pain

his gaze
it holds me
calms me
makes me born
anew

then suddenly i gasp
can look no more
can not escape
the throes that pierce
the struggle just to breathe
the sense that
with my blood
my very life
now drips onto the ground below

fallen from his gaze
i gasp
cannot go on
can breathe no more

but i no longer dread
the moment
finally
come

for i have risen from the cross

the sun

the sun had sparkled to its height
and for a moment halted wondering
if i topple
as i might
mine would be a cosmic blundering

and so it chose to shed its light
upon the endless drifting sand
and lest it topple
as it might
it chose to shine on through the land

then it started retrospecting
if i'd stayed to shed my light
upon the sand
its life reflecting
i might have toppled
yes
i might

carver of a tree

one night
i met a wandering likeness
of myself

its hand stretched out before me
and beckoned me to stay

i wavered
wondered
watched

then as i saw the hand recede
from the tree where it had slaved
i saw my life
carved out before me

for a while
i merely stood
and stared

then as i turned to walk away
i looked back
toward the tree
and through the night
i strained to see

but saw no likeness
saw no tree

and what was it
carved on a tree

had it been me

yet surely i
am not just me
not just an image on a tree

and as i plodded on my way
unsure of what i'd seen
i wondered if that hand
that carved my life
belonged to me

yet if that hand was mine
and if that likeness me
had i not carved the hand
that carved the life
that had been me

for surely i
am not just me
not just the carvings on a tree

and so i wrestled
with a heightened sense of me
as not just image
but as carver of a tree

father if this cup might pass away

i was born of woman
kind woman
caressing
soft
she called me son
i kissed her in return
and gave to her a golden coin

the dusty hillsides
camels' dung
the sweat of harems
knew them all
i knew them all
and loved them

i met a stranger once
he dressed in camel's hair
unbathed
his hair unkempt
he clambered in the sultry air
and said
pass on the golden coin

i knew him
loved him
saw him to the axe
and bled to death

and missed his
word made flesh

by a pond i stopped
stared
saw my image dangled by the sun
and floating on the placid spume
alone
a great one
trembling

i strolled along a shore
saw strangers make their catch
then shun all worth
for what they craved
yet couldn't grasp

we sauntered through the dusty highways
roadsides
parched of tongue
and out of breath
sat
were spoken to
and spoke

words
they fell like bones
to broken stone
were picked up
handled
buried
said a prayer or two
or tossed aside
to fertilize the soil

i crumbled to a rock
felt its keenness cut my will

my blood flowed freely
down the rocks
and through the crevices

i found a golden coin
golden coin golden coin
i found a golden coin
in the drylands
of my memory

i washed this golden coin
golden coin golden coin
i washed this golden coin
and watched it sparkle
it was heavenly

but i've lost my golden coin
golden coin golden coin
but i've lost my golden coin
and now it seems just like as any

father
if
this
cup
might
pass
away

yet
it's
a
way
i
cannot
keep
away

it
is
for
me
and
me
alone
to
walk

i pulled up from this altar
felt a pain or two
wiped my moistened eyes
cut into the setting sun a face

it was a long
and dreary contest
as the cosmos clamped its shell
around this feeble ruin

i mourned the loss
of what i'd been
of what i'd seen
of what i'd felt
as me

then saw
in the distance
calm
contented
sucking at its mother's breast
an infant
and was glad
and knew that i had done it
and had died
alone

but yes would do it
yes
would do it even now
again

nowhere to stay

i met you
sleeping quietly among the shrubs and boughs
in the wistful slumber
of a forest nymph

i saw eternity in your silent eyes
that tears had tread upon your tender cheeks
there was no withered
thought-worn
brow

i think i loved that moment
though no more than you
i know i loved that moment
it was you

time has trudged its weary path
it might have happened in a roman bower
or on the top of an etruscan tower
you might have kissed me on my cheek
you might have made me weep
time cradled you
i passed to my dotage

yet i know we'll share this moment
it may be mingled in a cup of sorrow
perhaps a handclasp on a dreary afternoon
it may be years before tomorrow
nor a moment of eternity too soon

it's not a dream i've dreamt so often
more a life i've lived for
day to day

i met you in a dream
you stole me in a solitary thought
you left nowhere to stay

my love is as the rose

i loved you all the summer through
amid the gentle autumn breezes
and into winter snows

then as the ice began to flow
and sparrows chirped their vernal song
you forgot to bloom

and should i sniff a withered rose

noah and the flood

the clouds are forming fast
but a moment till the deluge

all the animals have boarded
two by two

we'll last for forty days
or more
if all goes well

and the animals don't take sick
and the boards don't spring a leak

but tell me noah
what if

what if it doesn't rain

the ruins

its walls immense before me challenged my entrée
i flinched
then in a moment's vacillation
chose to stay

i wandered through its streets
and sighed in fear and trembling
i wandered through its alleyways
and stepped among the dangling limbs dissembling

i wandered through its park displays
and plucked its solitary flower
i wandered through its castles and its huts
and knew i would not live another hour

i wandered through its royal courts
and onward toward its multisplintered throne
i wandered through its dingy mausoleums
and on to where a lamp still faintly shone

i wandered through its latticed gates
and caught a fainting glimpse of its immenseness
i wandered through its memory and desire
and on to where i yearned for its intenseness

i wandered through its days
and through its nights
i wandered
till it crumbled from my sight

then i began to think
and wonder
whose were these lives and longings
torn asunder

for
i couldn't help but feel
they seemed much closer
and more real

not out there in the ruins
that i chose to see
but living deep within

inside of me

i know not what i do

i joined them
for a brief foray
into their inner worlds

could not embrace them
couldn't grace them
did not know how to stay

as they spoke of god the father
i longed for god
the mother

as they looked for mercy from without
i craved but mercy
from within

as they stood to state their faith
i could only stand
and wait

as they gave up all resistance
i could only share
my distance

and so i put them down
not wanting
them around

and looked at them as somehow less
not truly whole
not blessed

then as they left
i reached within myself
and felt a gentle longing

and as i felt it
so i sensed
that those whom i had faulted
were following
like me
but what to them
seemed heaven-sent

and then i felt
a sense of shame
at faulting those
whose only sin it was
to stay somewhere
beyond my willing ken

perhaps forgiveness is too late
yet now i have a place
for them
and for their longings too
for i share with them their fate

i know not what i do

liza lu

o liza lu
come out and play
your mother smiled and said you may

come out
the pony's waiting to be groomed
for you and me i know there's room

the kitty's fur has all grown back
and in the field are little tracks

along the fence some slats are broke
but please don't laugh
it's not a joke

a bird had fallen from its nest
it must have figured that was best

and in the yard's a little brook
which all the fishes have mistook

for up the brook a man and boy
are waiting for a catch
they'll both enjoy

and underneath the willow tree
there's grass for you
and grass for me

don't wait inside
you'll just be sad

and please come out
or i'll be mad

o liza lu
come out and play
i only have a moment left to stay

my china doll

once i owned a china doll

it had been given to me
by my father
on my seventh birthday

so closely did it resemble the statue of the virgin
in our parish church
that i proudly named it mary

but i had a thing about names

if something was called by a certain name
i didn't see the need to call it by that name
and so i didn't call my china doll mary
i was so afraid
deeply
interiorly
clandestinely
that if i called it mary
mary might begin to mean more to me
than my china doll

but i loved my father
who had given me my china doll

and i loved
or at this time at least liked
my china doll
and so i didn't call it mary

i cherished my china doll
above all my other possessions

my other toys i would pull out from my drawer
in the morning sunlight
to watch them come alive
before they were laid to rest
at dusk
exhausted from their full day of play

and they would play so vigorously
toy soldier fighting toy soldier
toy cowboy parleying with toy indian
toy sheriff subduing toy horse thief

i would sit for hours
passionately involved in their antics

i would observe a stagecoach driver
disobeying a stop sign in the middle of the prairie
even when indians weren't chasing him

i would see cowboys and soldiers
tell of heroic deeds
become drunk in an hour
and spend the night in jail

and once
i even saw squint-eyed thugs
casing a church

my heart thumped as they
having committed the perfect crime
rushed frenziedly from the sanctuary
like robbers in the night
laden with the gold of chalices and candlesticks

then my whole breath seemed suspended
while i watched my toy sheriff subdue them
shooting at them with bullets
that could only hurt a toy

they seemed so much like real people

but then
i was only a child
and in my childlike way
i delighted in their feigned adultness
in their joy at rising
in their sorrow over a common loss
in their prankishness
when i announced
that it was time
for all good toys
to return to their toy drawer

but there was one exception
my china doll
she was different

oh at first
i had to put her away
with all my other toys

then night after night
i would long for her

i would long to caress her china body
in the palms of my hands
to feel with my fingers
the figure of her china mold

i liked my china doll
i liked her very much
and
in time
i grew to love her

one day
when all my toys were playing
i talked alone to my china doll

we talked about just anything
for quite some time

before long
i knew i had something important to tell her
it wasn't just conversation
it was what my father used to call
tête-à-tête
and so i prepared myself to say it

i kind of blushed for a moment
but slowly
and resolutely
i asked my china doll
if she would marry me

for an instant
a moment i'll not forget
i think
she too

blushed

then
almost instantaneously
we burst into happiness
we shared a brief interlude of toy heaven
and i was filled with love

i'm sure not even alexander
as he gazed across the indus
could have more worthily borne the laurel wreathe
than i
enamoured by the pinhead bluish eyes
of my china doll

after this momentous conquest
i thought it prudent
to discuss our future plans

the most timely question was
how were we going to get married

of course
we could not elope
no
never
that would not be right
all the other toys would reject us
and then
then
a thought leaped forth which broke my childish heart
then they would no longer be my toys

you see
a toy is something one makes

a horse
a soldier
or a china doll
is nothing
and certainly not a toy
until i make it something for me

then they would no longer be my toys
and i would not hear of this

there was but one recourse
i would announce our engagement
to all the other toys
and then
since no one would feel slighted or belittled
all my toys could share my joy

it had been a hard day
a day of decisions
and my china doll and i were tired
and it was dusk
the time had come to say good night

my china doll begged me
to keep her out of the toy drawer

after all
she was special

i wanted to
oh how deeply i wanted to
but i just couldn't
i hadn't announced our engagement
to the other toys yet

i mean
to the toys

you see
a horse
a soldier
or a china doll
becomes more than a toy
once you have proposed
once you have made yourself something for it

my china doll was more than a toy
and yet i had to respect propriety
and so i told her
she would have to stay with the toys one more night

we smiled at each other
haloed in our happiness
then we kissed good night
and i laid her gently in the toy drawer

the next day
i announced the gospel of our love

my toys were thrilled
they had never seen a real
well almost real
wedding
like all toys
my toys shared only toy experiences
and so on that day
my toys and i celebrated

from that day on
i kept my china doll out of the toy drawer

of course we were only engaged
but
well
after all
she wasn't sleeping with
i mean
she slept alone
on the desk
in a toilet-tissue-padded matchbox bed
specially built for her

for many days
my toys and i were happy
and i was especially enchanted
with the shell-like presence
of my china doll

we talked a lot
we would discuss things like
when we would be married
how many children we would have
what kind of house we would live in

she never once seemed troubled
that i didn't show her more of the house
than my bedroom
i guessed it was her woman's intuition
which secretly revealed to her
what the rest of a real house was like

once a queer
almost philosophical thought
jumped into my head

since

after all
i was real
and my china doll was of china
what would our children be
real children
or toy children of china
but
in my reverie
i passed on to more timely subjects
and then we played together
and had fun

at last my day of glory came
i had waited for it
it must have been a lifetime
all my seven years

my china doll and i didn't talk much that day
we seemed to have learned
that words were not enough

at last
out of our sea of silence
i issued a faint ripple of words

i asked my china doll
if she would sleep with me that night

there
for the second time since i had known her
i think my china doll blushed
but it passed as quickly as it came
and left us filled with joy

when at length
night fell

i put my toys away
then slid between my covers
and gently cushioned my china doll
within the folds of my pillow

there she lay
as in marble relief
with the delicacy of a toy masterwork
and i the toy artisan

for many days thereafter
i left her alone
on my desk

i was so afraid
that i might lie on her
during the night
and break her china mold

then came a day
it was a dreadful day
it was lightening
and thundering
and hailing

it was making a dreadful racket
and you can imagine how my little toys felt
since i
their lord and master
was so frightened

thus it was that my beloved china doll
requested that i put her back into the toy drawer
with all the other toys

in their company

she would not be nearly as frightened

i was grieved that my beloved
should prefer the company of all the toys
to mine
in this time of trial
but
after all
she did sleep alone
on the desk
in a matchbox bed padded with toilet paper

i understood

i kissed her good night
though my heart was sad
and placed her on top of the toys

the following morning arrived
i had slept little that night
and was now breathlessly excited
to see my china doll

in my childish delight
i kicked the covers from my bed
ran over to the toy drawer

i skipped part of the way
because i stubbed my toe
on a nightstand
beside my bed

heaved it open

for a moment
the first time since i had had my toys

i had gotten them on christmas
a few months before my birthday
when i got my china doll

or rather
since they had become my toys

and they really were my toys
they played for me
they lived for me
they fought for me

not a word was spoken
no
good morning
no
did you sleep well last night
no
here is our master
bringing to us
the dawn of day

all was silent

it's funny how
at times of sympathy and quiet
my toys would change their masks

you see
each toy had a wardrobe of hundreds of masks
a face to put on for each occasion
each meeting with another toy

a friend
my uncle who died last year

once said
all people are afflicted
with a sense of tragedy
which comes alive for them
in their moments
of profoundest experience
he didn't say if this applied to toys
but i think they're just like people

i guessed i knew what my uncle meant
that people aren't really people
until they've been deprived of something
or someone
special

then my uncle went on to say
that at the apex of a tragic experience
is a moment of sheer comedy
but when i was five and my brother died
i didn't want to laugh
when i was six
and my cat caught his head in a tin can
and bled to death trying to get out
i was deeply moved
in fact
i cried
and so i guessed my uncle was wrong

at the apex of a tragic experience
is a moment of sheer sorrow
but here i was
trying to sound like a philosopher
and i was really just a child
and so i kind of laughed when i said this
i mean

the thing about sheer sorrow
somehow it seemed too somber
and i wasn't prepared to accept it
but i had begun to feel alone
for there was no one to share my moment
of quiet tragedy

my toys around me were silent

but there i was
trying to get away from myself

my eyes were really filled with tears
my heart pressed hard against my entrails
for there
through my warm tears
i saw my china doll
but she was no longer smiling

i knew this was the end
of the engagement
of the smiles
of the happy times

there
on the bottom of the drawer
my trembling hand
caressed a heap of broken china
become moist with my cataract of tears

for a moment
i lost my balance
fell upon the opened drawer
and cried

then slowly
as i raised my body
i rolled my tear-streaked eyes
over the assemblage of toys

voiceless
though not breathless
a toy soldier

actually he was an army sergeant like my dad
because i could see his sergeant stripes
and his helmet
and

well he said that i had placed my china doll
on the back of a horse
an immense horse
a big white stallion
and that
since my china doll knew nothing of
of
of horsemanship

he cleared his throat and continued

she fell from a horse last night
and
well

his voice wavered

there was nothing we could do
we're deeply sorry

as i stared

fixated by the dim light
bending through my window
my heart was heavy
with the anguish
of a child's paradise lost

i went into mourning

i must have left my toys
in the drawer that day
for the first time since i had gotten them
and for many days to come

about a week later
maybe it was two
i don't remember
my toys and i buried my beloved china doll

we had a modest procession
from my drawer
across my room
to the window

there my toy priest said mass
and recited in his latin accent
may mary rest in peace

what
my head pounded
i could not believe it
i jumped up
no
no
i cried
please don't call her mary

i mean
i know that was her name
but
it was really my china doll
that died last week

then i almost thought i saw my china doll
rise from her bier
in the center aisle of my toy church
and slowly and serenely
disappear
amidst a cloud of vapor
and i knew i was alone
but i was not lonely
i had my toys

my toys and i prayed
that she had gone to toy heaven
and if it was anything
like the moments i shared with her
well
i knew she was happy
she just had to be
and it almost made me smile to think of it
but i felt a pain in my head
where i had bruised myself
falling from my bed the other night
and i heard footsteps
my nurse's
and knew that my toys and i
would have to hurry
and so we placed the remains
of my china doll
in an earth-filled flower pot
which i kept on my window sill

in the sunlight
and watered every day

the party

her voice approached
and with a hand
it carved into the smoke-filled room
its note of doom

she spoke abruptly
you've come to me to party
here you'll find the tea and crumpets
over there the cards
i've done with sounding trumpets
and the revelry of bards
this party is a quiet one
or we'll have dispersed
before the setting sun has immersed

the party droned with multitudes of muddled thoughts
and in my corner of the bog
i felt a lonely drifting log in a wilderness of sea
then her gesture turned toward me

i made my faint crescendo
to lay an arm upon her shoulder
but from sighs and innuendo

surmised she was much colder
it was like a dream gone mad
we joked and talked
but i was sad and walked away
i'd grown much older

a lover's summer's spring

it is spring
i plant my flowers now

you plant yours too
there is room
in the neighbor's empty lot

maybe we can even build a wall
to protect them

what
you say you lost your hoe
you misplaced it in the autumn rains

i am so sorry
i need mine for myself
and for my flowers too

perhaps next spring we can plant together
meanwhile
have a lover's summer's spring

days

as our days pass
brief or long
we dream of what we might create
but do we make a song

no more

she touched me with her eyes
held me with her look
she doffed her smock
said smilingly
farewell
she spoke of love
and fondled me

her breath against my flesh
her body warm and supple
we touched
caressed
and swellingly embraced
then all too soon uncoupled

we lay inert
but for the rhythm of our chests
then slowly
limply
parted from our rest

and as we put back on
the trappings of our roles
we knew we had not

even for a moment
shared the contours of our souls

what might this have been
had we but shared a little more
of what was in us
deep within
and not just viscous in its form

yet we did not
would not
share a little more
and now we are not
no we are not
now we are no more

listen

listen to the son
he's mine
and in the radiance of his face
will shine
a glimmering of everlasting grace

you heard him say
blessed be the poor
who seek a priceless pearl
for when at length they find it
they waken in another world

listen to the son
he's mine
and in the radiance of his face
will shine
a glimmering of everlasting grace

you heard him say
blessed be the mourning
who've lost a friend or cat or leaf
for they will find their comfort
out beyond their grief

listen to the son
he's mine
and in the radiance of his face
will shine
a glimmering of everlasting grace

you heard him say
blessed be the pure in heart
who see not pain and sorrow
for when they stop to take a look
they see a new tomorrow

listen to the son
he's mine
and in the radiance of his face
will shine
a glimmering of everlasting grace

you heard him say
blessed be the peacemakers
who what they now abhor
set right by reaching out
not war

listen to the son
he's mine
and in the radiance of his face
will shine
a glimmering of everlasting grace

you heard him say
blessed be the . . .

never mind

you're not listening

christus imperat[2]

christus vincit
they shouted as they raised their banner
christus regnat
in their accustomed certain manner
they cursed
and shrieked
forgive them not
christus imperat

and tell me
neighbor
christus vincit
do you shout
do you raise your banner
christus regnat
are you certain in your manner
do you forgive
or do you not
christus imperat

---

[2] The poem's title is taken from "Christus vincit, Christus regnat, Christus imperat" ("Christ conquers, Christ reigns, Christ commands"), a medieval Gregorian chant.

it was a long and painful road
from court to rocky knoll
he must have fallen several times
from sheer exhaustion
once
i have heard it said
a stranger wiped his brow
and in this moment
saw the face of one
who *vincit*
but without a banner
regnat
in a gentle manner
and in this way
christlike
imperat

his mother's womb

suffocating on a cross
fleshly
bloodily embossed

hanging openly
caressing
in word and gesture blessing

then gasping
in a painful union
a shrieking mortally communion

lifeless now
yet oddly living
in this final act of giving

his followers soon took him down
laid him gently on the ground
then washed him
wrapped him
laid him in a tomb
his final resting place
his mother's womb

dark night of the soul

i wandered through the desert
was eaten by the sun

the sand
it beckoned me

bent low to drink from my mirage
i wept

my tears
they were no solace

weak of frame
i craved a carven idol to caress

but all i found was
sand

you

empty as a freshly dug hole
that awaits a seed
i say to you . . .

wondering how we strayed
so long ago
from our walk through life together
i say to you . . .

wishing we were one person
uniting organs in a single body
i say to you . . .

hoping your walk through life was friendly
with enough of what you longed for
i say to you . . .

regretting times when
pulled by our ends
we walked apart
i say to you . . .

caressing moments that warmed us
and molded all our days
i say to you . . .

in the light and the dark
in the full and the empty

i remember you

moments

death
is but a moment
of a life

life
is but a moment
of a death

as we live
and die
the moments
that we are
we live our deaths
and die our lives
endlessly

yet only for a moment

a tear

one day i felt a tear

from where it came
i did not know

puzzled by the lineage
of that intrepid guest
i looked around
but not a sight leapt forth
nor sound

the object of my grief
hoping still to see
i looked into the tear itself

and there i saw but me

having

you sought your having
not your being
so you did not be
and now you do not have

the mourner

a spider was weaving her web
in the corner of the sash
i asked if i might watch from my bed
she shot forth like a lightening flash
though she said not a word
a look which inferred
that of course she was going to demur

then she ran to the corner
and i
like a mourner
stood plainly
my heart in my head

with a breeze from the north
i walked silently forth
and lay down to rest on my bed

the i i am

i who am this i i am
am not just who i am

who i am
i am

and yet i am not who i am
who i am not
i am

who am i then
this i i am

i am who am and am not i

my favorite witch[3]

you shared profoundly
spoke and laughed and sometimes cried
were totally engrossed

you loved your mother nature
and all her children near and far
you lived the rhythms of her life

you asked me if i loved you
and my reply was yes
to share so much so deeply
had to bring us close

you gave me depth
by laying bare your longings and your fears
and there will always be a space within me
for your tears

of all the things that I could say
only one will keep you safe

---

[3]   This poem is dedicated to someone I once knew who practiced Wicca.

to always trust yourself

though other lights will shine
and beckon you to stay
only you can light your way

dead and laughing

say farewell to life
you mere shadow of a man

will you haunt these parts
forever

be gone
to your happy hunting ground

perhaps on that ground
you can take without defacing

perhaps beyond the reach of men
you'll find your manhood

you didn't find it here
among the living

may you laugh among the dead

looking and listening and longing

i look for you
i long for you
where are you
where am i now
that we are no more
we are not more
we are not
yet we are

she was several years younger than i
had grown up in another town
had run away from home

when i met her
she lived with a couple guys
slept in the same bed as one of them
but insisted he was impotent
and
since he and others said so too
i guessed it was probably true

i found her attractive
and
as far as i could tell
she seemed to like me too

although we were around each other often
at parties
at the house where she lived
in the student union
we had not gone out together

then i moved away

i saw her
off and on
over the next year
whenever i was back in town

i even thought about asking her
to stay with me
but by then she was living with a foster family
had a job she seemed to like
and so i never asked

our relationship
begun as friendship
had evolved into much more

she filled an emptiness in me

i want you
how i want you
how i want you to want
not anything
or anyone
but me
only me
in this moment
of my longing

it was finally summer
i had finished my courses
and decided to spend some time back home

i saw her
as soon as i got back

but when i knocked on her door
a couple days later
there was no answer

i knocked again
no answer
again
no answer
again
no answer

i went by her house
and called
many times
over the next few days

someone
finally
answered the door
said she wasn't there
had gone

i asked around
but no one seemed to know where she was

the days
and weeks

passed

everywhere i went
i looked for her

i could not enter a room
or see a group of people
without looking
intently
to see if she was there

for many months
i looked for her
and longed for her

i never saw her again

at this time in my life
i often went on walks
and when i walked
in the evening
after dark
i always noticed the houses along the way
and what
if anything
was happening
in and around them

sometimes i saw nothing
sometimes someone was sitting on a porch
sometimes people were talking in the front or back yard
sometimes they said hello
once i saw an elderly lady
through her front screen door
on a hot summer night

watching tv
as she lay naked on her couch

i always felt a sense of peace
and belonging
as i walked casually along
and
in my distant way
embraced the lives of those i saw and heard

much of my walk through life has been like this
casually observing
while respecting
the lives of others

but now my walk through life was different

for many months
i wandered
through its streets
and alleys
looking
and listening
and longing

i look for you
i long for you
where are you
where am i now
that we are no more
we are not more
we are not
yet we are

i

i am
and i am i
within me
am what is

who am i then
if i am i
i am who am
who yet am i

yet i am not
i am beyond me
am what is not
am not i

who am i if
i am not i
i am who am not
am not i

who am i then
who am i if
i am who am
and am not i

no one's looking

but mother
no one's looking
and i laughed
no one's looking
but mother
no one's looking
and i sighed
no one's looking
but mother
no one's looking
and i felt
no one's looking
but mother
no one's looking
and i saw
no one's looking
but mother
no one's looking
and i gasped
no one's looking
but mother
no one's looking
and i cried
no one's looking

but mother
no one's looking
and i shouted
no one's looking
but mother
no one's looking
and i screamed
no one's looking

then fell silent

as i died

with
no
one
looking

falling

i am one falling

i fall from no origin
i fall to no destination

arms outstretched
in an eternal embrace
i merely fall

i hope for no end
i regret no loss

if only one person
would extend a hand
that i might not merely fall
but
for a fleeting moment
coincide

and be my flesh

and be my spirit

and be my life

CPSIA information can be obtained
at www.ICGtesting.com
Printed in the USA
BVHW031415150419
545532BV00002B/43/P